KATHLEEN KRULL

ILLUSTRATED BY

DAVID DIAZ

WILMA
UNLIMITED

How Wilma Rudolph Became the World's Fastest Woman

HARCOURT BRACE & COMPANY

San Diego   New York   London

Requests for permission to make copies of any part of the work should be mailed to: Permissions Department,
Harcourt Brace & Company, 6277 Sea Harbor Drive, Orlando, Florida 32887-6777.

Photographs by David Diaz and Cecelia Zieba-Diaz

Library of Congress Cataloging-in-Publication Data
Krull, Kathleen.
Wilma unlimited: how Wilma Rudolph became the world's fastest woman/Kathleen Krull;
illustrated by David Diaz.
p.   cm.
Summary: A biography of the African American woman who overcame crippling polio as a child to become the first
woman to win three gold medals in track in a single Olympics.
ISBN 0-15-201267-2
1. Rudolph, Wilma, 1940–1994—Juvenile literature.   2. Runners (Sports)—United States—
Biography—Juvenile literature.
[1. Rudolph, Wilma, 1940–1994.   2. Track-and-field athletes.   3. Afro-Americans—Biography.   4. Women—
Biography.]   I. Diaz, David, ill.   II. Title.
GV1061.15.R83K78   1996
796.42'092—dc20
[B]   95-32105
F G

Printed in Singapore

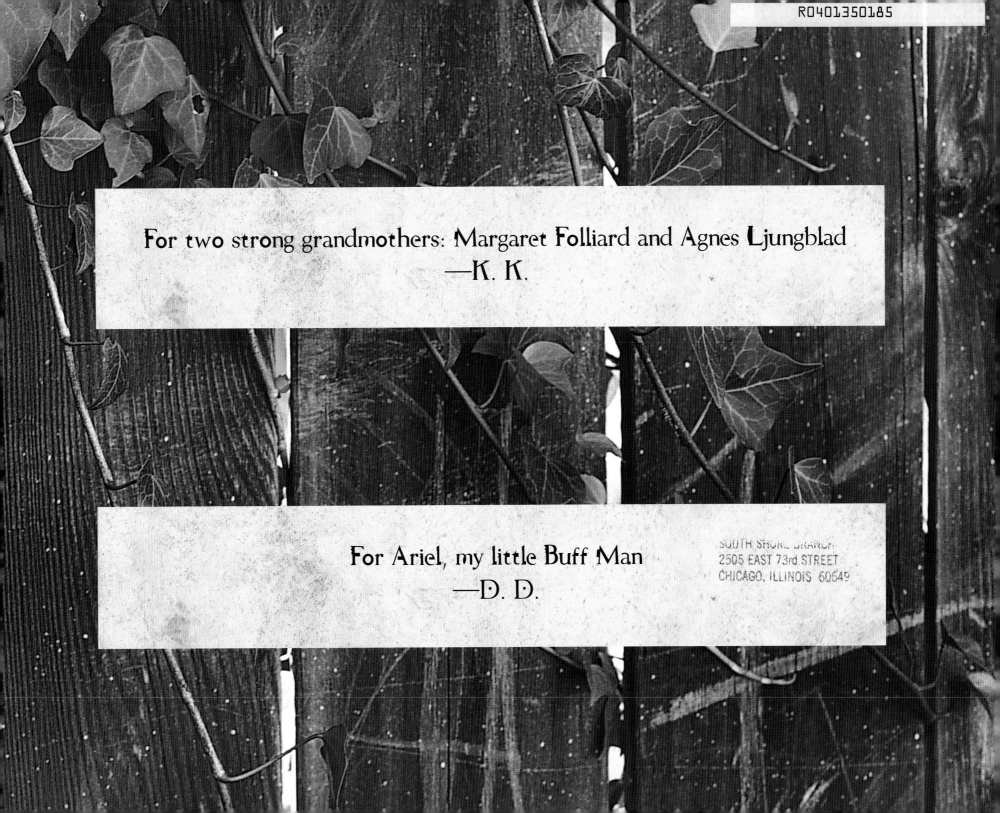

For two strong grandmothers: Margaret Folliard and Agnes Ljungblad
—K. K.

For Ariel, my little Buff Man
—D. D.

No one expected such a tiny girl to have a first birthday. In Clarksville, Tennessee, in 1940, life for a baby who weighed just over four pounds at birth was sure to be limited.

But most babies didn't have nineteen older brothers and sisters to watch over them. Most babies didn't have a mother who knew home remedies and a father who worked several jobs.

Most babies weren't Wilma Rudolph.

Wilma did celebrate her first birthday, and everyone noticed that as soon as this girl could walk, she ran or jumped instead.

She worried people, though—she was always so small and sickly. If a brother or sister had a cold, she got double pneumonia. If one of them had measles, Wilma got measles, too, plus mumps and chicken pox.

Her mother always nursed her at home. Doctors were a luxury for the Rudolph family, and anyway, only one doctor in Clarksville would treat black people.

Just before Wilma turned five, she got sicker than ever. Her sisters and brothers heaped all the family's blankets on her, trying to keep her warm.

During that sickness, Wilma's left leg twisted inward, and she couldn't move it back. Not even Wilma's mother knew what was wrong.

The doctor came to see her then. Besides scarlet fever, he said, Wilma had also been stricken with polio. In those days, most children who got polio either died or were permanently crippled. There was no cure.

The news spread around Clarksville: Wilma, that lively girl, would never walk again.

But Wilma kept moving any way she could. By hopping on one foot, she could get herself around the house, to the outhouse in the backyard, and even, on Sundays, to church.

Wilma's mother urged her on. Mrs. Rudolph had plenty to do — cooking, cleaning, sewing patterned flour sacks into clothes for her children, now twenty-two in all. Yet twice every week, she and Wilma took the bus to the nearest hospital that would treat black patients, some fifty miles away in Nashville. They rode together in the back, the only place blacks were allowed to sit.

Doctors and nurses at the hospital helped Wilma do exercises to make her paralyzed leg stronger. At home, Wilma practiced them constantly, even when it hurt.

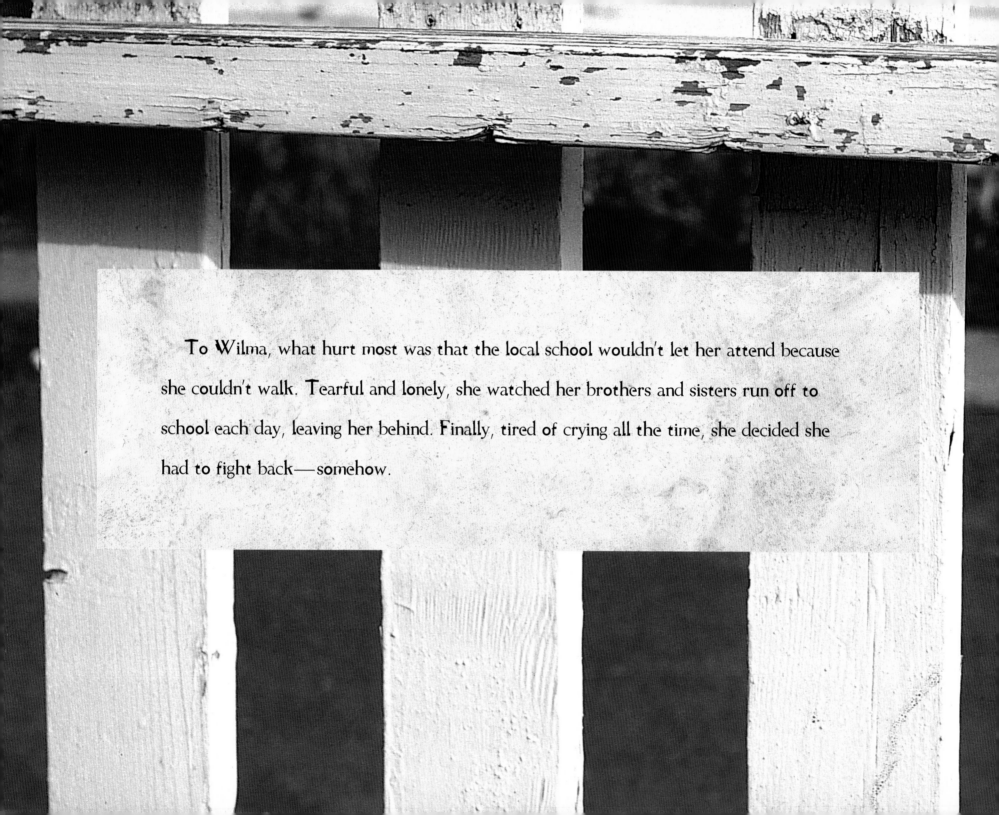

To Wilma, what hurt most was that the local school wouldn't let her attend because she couldn't walk. Tearful and lonely, she watched her brothers and sisters run off to school each day, leaving her behind. Finally, tired of crying all the time, she decided she had to fight back—somehow.

Wilma worked so hard at her exercises that the doctors decided she was ready for a heavy steel brace. With the brace supporting her leg, she didn't have to hop anymore. School was possible at last.

But it wasn't the happy place she had imagined. Her classmates made fun of her brace. During playground games she could only sit on the sidelines, twitchy with impatience. She studied the other kids for hours—memorizing moves, watching the ball zoom through the rim of the bushel basket they used as a hoop.

Wilma fought the sadness by doing more leg exercises. Her family always cheered her on, and Wilma did everything she could to keep them from worrying about her. At times her leg really did seem to be getting stronger. Other times it just hurt.

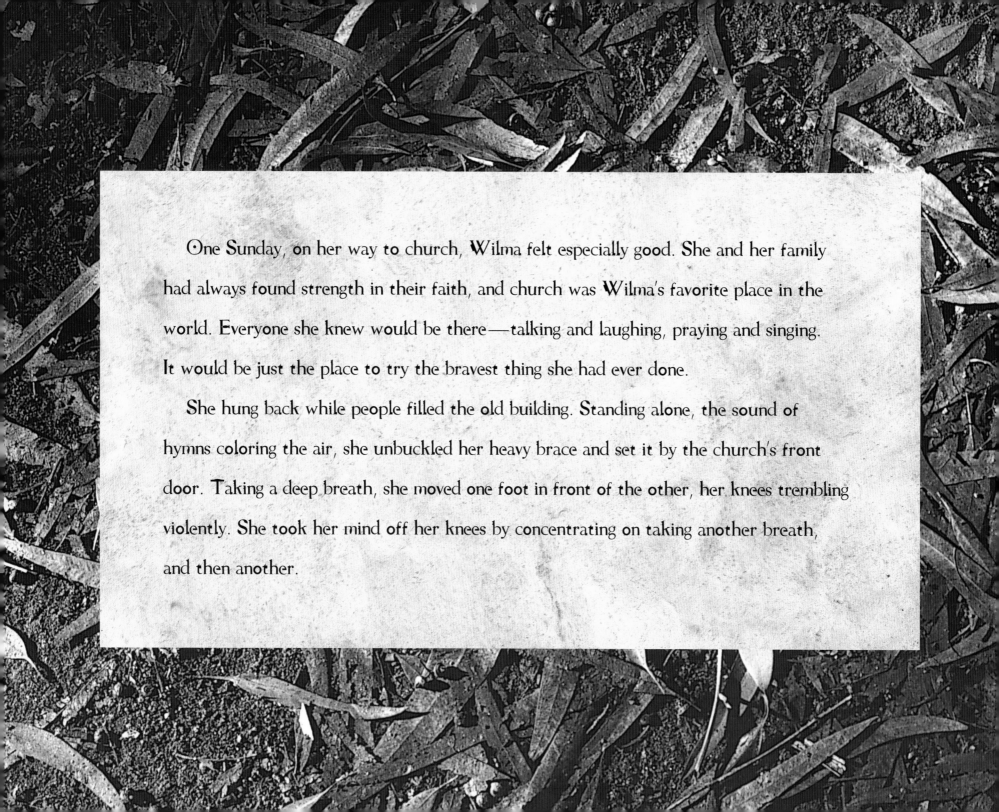

One Sunday, on her way to church, Wilma felt especially good. She and her family had always found strength in their faith, and church was Wilma's favorite place in the world. Everyone she knew would be there—talking and laughing, praying and singing. It would be just the place to try the bravest thing she had ever done.

She hung back while people filled the old building. Standing alone, the sound of hymns coloring the air, she unbuckled her heavy brace and set it by the church's front door. Taking a deep breath, she moved one foot in front of the other, her knees trembling violently. She took her mind off her knees by concentrating on taking another breath, and then another.

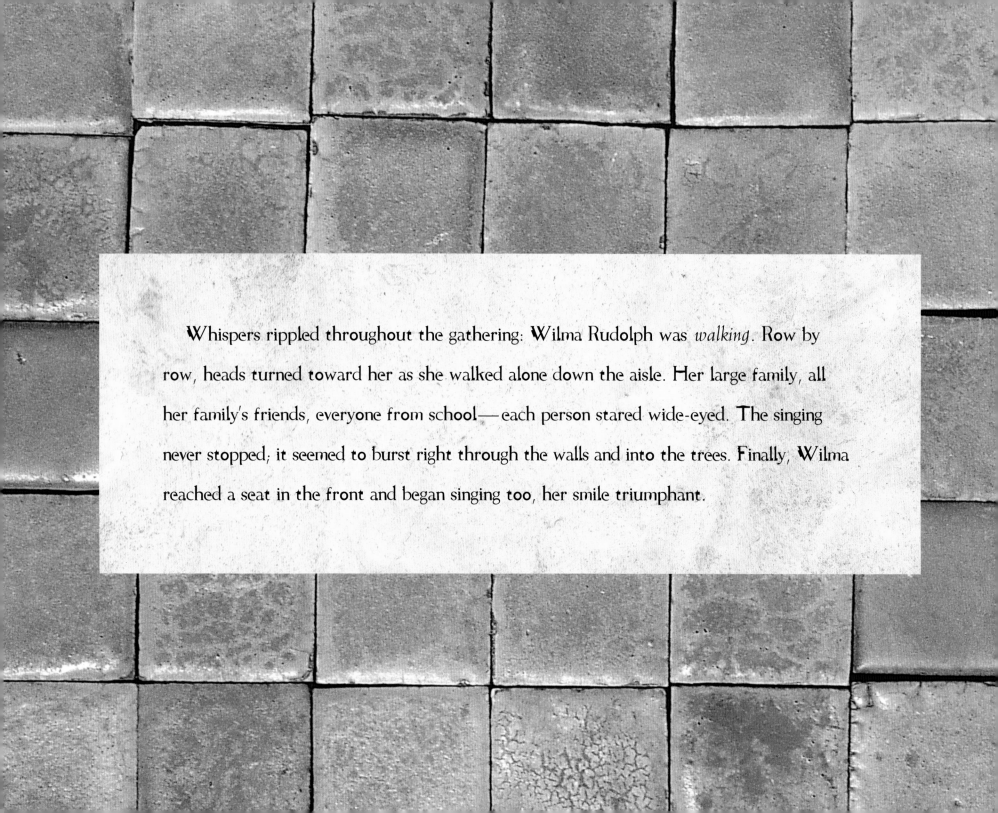

Whispers rippled throughout the gathering: Wilma Rudolph was *walking*. Row by row, heads turned toward her as she walked alone down the aisle. Her large family, all her family's friends, everyone from school—each person stared wide-eyed. The singing never stopped; it seemed to burst right through the walls and into the trees. Finally, Wilma reached a seat in the front and began singing *too*, her smile triumphant.

Wilma practiced walking as often as she could after that, and when she was twelve years old, she was able to take off the brace for good. She and her mother realized she could get along without it, so one memorable day, they wrapped the hated brace in a box and mailed it back to the hospital.

As soon as Wilma sent that box away, she knew her life was beginning all over again.

After years of sitting on the sidelines, Wilma couldn't wait to throw herself into basketball, the game she had most liked to watch. She was skinny but no longer tiny. Her long, long legs would propel her across the court and through the air, and she knew all the rules and all the moves.

In high school, she led her basketball team to one victory after another. Eventually, she took the team all the way to the Tennessee state championships. There, to everyone's astonishment, her team lost.

Wilma had become accustomed to winning. Now she slumped on the bench, all the liveliness knocked out of her.

But at the game that day was a college coach. He admired Wilma's basketball playing but was especially impressed by the way she ran. He wanted her for his track-and-field team.

With his help, Wilma won a full athletic scholarship to Tennessee State University. She was the first member of her family to go to college.

Eight years after she mailed her brace away, Wilma's long legs and years of hard work carried her thousands of miles from Clarksville, Tennessee. The summer of 1960 she arrived in Rome, Italy, to represent the United States at the Olympic Games—as a runner.

Just participating in the Olympics was a deeply personal victory for Wilma, but her chances of winning a race were limited. Simply walking in Rome's shimmering heat was a chore, and athletes from other countries had run faster races than Wilma ever had. Women weren't thought to run very well, anyway; track-and-field was considered a sport for men. And the pressure from the public was intense—for the first time ever, the Olympics would be shown on television, and all the athletes knew that more than one hundred million people would be watching. Worst of all, Wilma had twisted her ankle just after she arrived in Rome. It was still swollen and painful on the day of her first race.

Yet once it was her turn to compete, Wilma forgot her ankle and everything else. She lunged forward, not thinking about her fear, her pain, or the sweat flying off her face. She ran better than she ever had before. And she ran better than anyone else.

Grabbing the attention of the whole world, Wilma Rudolph of the United States won the 100-meter dash. No one else even came close. An Olympic gold medal was hers to take home.

So when it was time for the 200-meter dash, Wilma's graceful long legs were already famous. Her ears buzzed with the sound of the crowd chanting her name. Such support helped her ignore the rain that was beginning to fall. At the crack of the starting gun, she surged into the humid air like a tornado. When she crossed the finish line, she had done it again. She finished far ahead of everyone else. She had earned her second gold medal. Wet and breathless, Wilma was exhilarated by the double triumph. The crowd went wild.

The 400-meter relay race was yet to come. Wilma's team faced the toughest competition of all. And as the fourth and final runner on her team, it was Wilma who had to cross the finish line.

Wilma's teammates ran well, passed the baton smoothly, and kept the team in first place. Wilma readied herself for the dash to the finish line as her third teammate ran toward her. She reached back for the baton—and nearly dropped it. As she tried to recover from the fumble, two other runners sped past her. Wilma and her team were suddenly in third place.

Ever since the day she had walked down the aisle at church, Wilma had known the power of concentration. Now, legs pumping, she put her mind to work. In a final, electrifying burst of speed, she pulled ahead. By a fraction of a second, she was the first to blast across the finish line. The thundering cheers matched the thundering of her own heart. She had made history. She had won for an astounding third time.

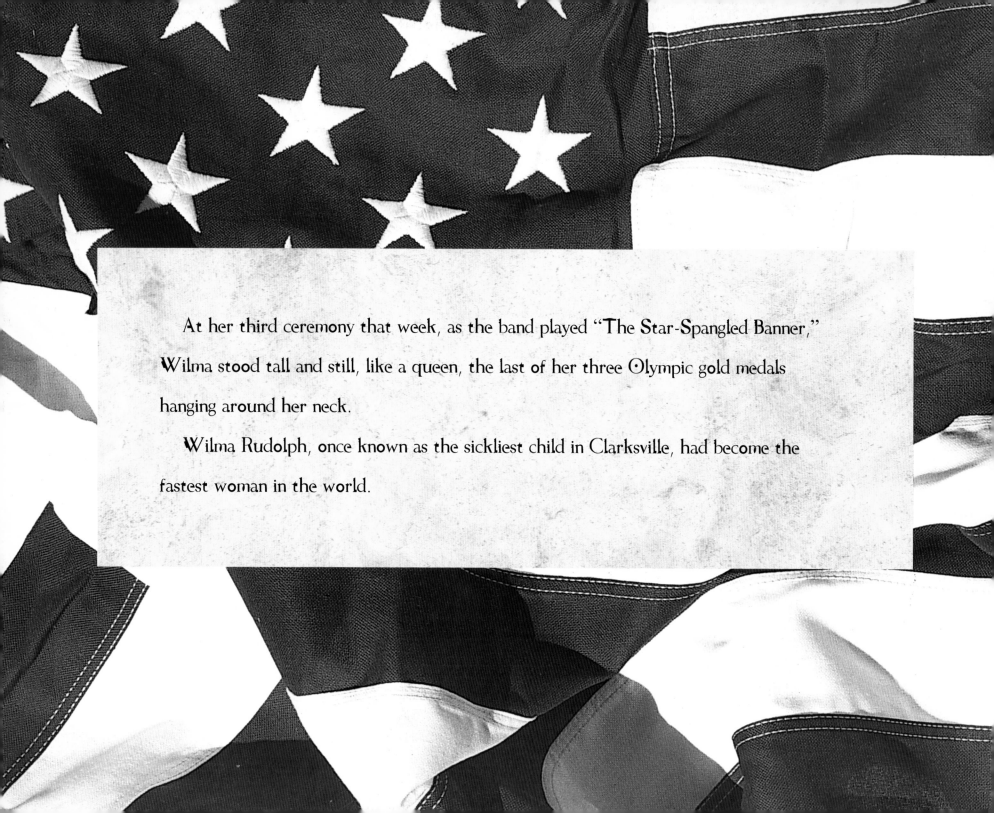

At her third ceremony that week, as the band played "The Star-Spangled Banner," Wilma stood tall and still, like a queen, the last of her three Olympic gold medals hanging around her neck.

Wilma Rudolph, once known as the sickliest child in Clarksville, had become the fastest woman in the world.

AUTHOR'S NOTE

Wilma Rudolph became, at age twenty, the first American woman to win three gold medals at a single Olympics. When she returned home from Rome, her family was waiting for her, and so was all of Clarksville, Tennessee. The huge parade and banquet held in her honor were the first events in the town's history to include both blacks and whites.

During the time of Wilma's childhood in the 1940s, polio, also known as infantile paralysis, was the world's most dreaded disease. A cure for it was not found until 1955. By then it had killed or crippled 357,000 Americans, mostly children—only 50,000 fewer than the number of Americans who had died in World War II.

After she retired from her career as a runner in 1962, Wilma became a second-grade teacher and a high school coach. She remained a much-admired celebrity, but to prove that there was more to her than just running, she started a company called Wilma Unlimited that gave her opportunities to travel, lecture, and support causes she believed in. Later she founded the nonprofit Wilma Rudolph Foundation to nurture young athletes and to teach them that they, too, can succeed despite all odds against them. The story of all she overcame in order to win at the Olympics has inspired thousands of young athletes, especially women.

Wilma Rudolph died in 1994.

The paintings in this book were created with acrylics, watercolor, and gouache on Arches watercolor paper.

The backgrounds were composed and photographed by David Diaz and Cecelia Zieba-Diaz.

The display type and text type were set in Ariel, a font created by David Diaz.

Color separations by Bright Arts, Ltd., Singapore

Printed and bound by Tien Wah Press, Singapore

Production supervision by Stanley Redfern

Designed by David Diaz with special assistance from Cecelia Zieba-Diaz and Troy Viss

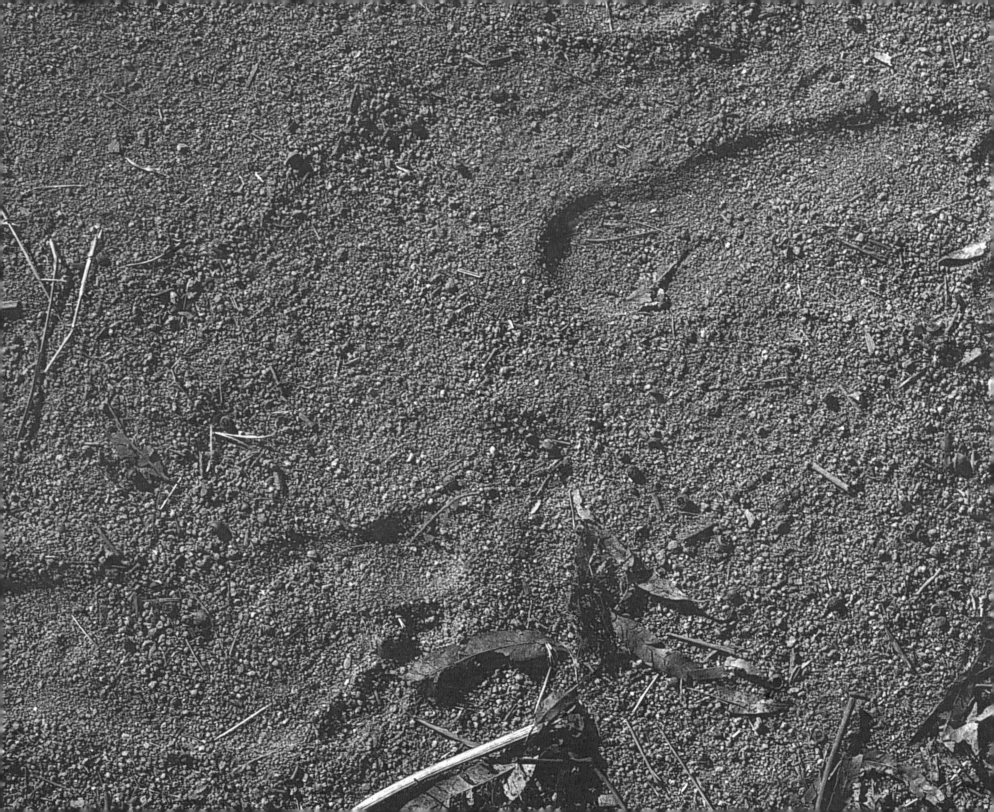